BLUE BANNER
BIOGRAPHY

# PITBULL

*Risa Brown*

Mitchell Lane

PUBLISHERS

P.O. Box 196
Hockessin, Delaware 19707
Visit us on the web: www.mitchelllane.com
Comments? Email us: mitchelllane@mitchelllane.com

**Mitchell Lane**
PUBLISHERS

Printing    1        2        3        4        5        6        7        8        9

### Blue Banner Biographies

| | | |
|---|---|---|
| Abby Wambach | Ice Cube | Miguel Tejada |
| Adele | Ja Rule | Mike Trout |
| Alicia Keys | Jamie Foxx | Nancy Pelosi |
| Allen Iverson | Jason Derulo | Natasha Bedingfield |
| Ashanti | Jay-Z | Nicki Minaj |
| Ashlee Simpson | Jennifer Hudson | One Direction |
| Ashton Kutcher | Jennifer Lopez | Orianthi |
| Avril Lavigne | Jessica Simpson | Orlando Bloom |
| Blake Lively | J. K. Rowling | P. Diddy |
| Blake Shelton | Joe Flacco | Peyton Manning |
| Bow Wow | John Legend | Pink |
| Brett Favre | Justin Berfield | Pitbull |
| Britney Spears | Justin Timberlake | Prince William |
| Bruno Mars | Kanye West | Queen Latifah |
| CC Sabathia | Kate Hudson | Rihanna |
| Carrie Underwood | Katy Perry | Robert Downey Jr. |
| Chris Brown | Keith Urban | Robert Pattinson |
| Chris Daughtry | Kelly Clarkson | Ron Howard |
| Christina Aguilera | Kenny Chesney | Sean Kingston |
| Ciara | Ke$ha | Selena |
| Clay Aiken | Kevin Durant | Shakira |
| Cole Hamels | Kristen Stewart | Shia LaBeouf |
| Condoleezza Rice | Lady Gaga | Shontelle Layne |
| Corbin Bleu | Lance Armstrong | Soulja Boy Tell 'Em |
| Daniel Radcliffe | Leona Lewis | Stephenie Meyer |
| David Ortiz | Lil Wayne | Taylor Swift |
| David Wright | Lionel Messi | T.I. |
| Derek Jeter | Lindsay Lohan | Timbaland |
| Drew Brees | LL Cool J | Tim McGraw |
| Eminem | Ludacris | Tim Tebow |
| Eve | Mariah Carey | Toby Keith |
| Fergie | Mario | Usher |
| Flo Rida | Mary J. Blige | Vanessa Anne Hudgens |
| Gwen Stefani | Mary-Kate and Ashley Olsen | Will.i.am |
| Hope Solo | Megan Fox | Zac Efron |

**Library of Congress Cataloging-in-Publication Data**
Brown, Risa W.
Pitbull / by Risa Brown.
      pages cm. — (Blue banner biographies)
Includes bibliographical references and index.
ISBN 978-1-61228-644-0 (library bound)
1. Pitbull (Rapper)—Juvenile literature. 2. Rap musicians—United States—Biography—Juvenile literature. I. Title.
ML3930.P48B76 2015
782.421649092—dc23
[B]
                                                                          2014020458
eBook ISBN: 9781612286686

**ABOUT THE AUTHOR:** Risa Brown is the author of twelve books for children and three for librarians. She has been a children's or school librarian for twenty-three years. She now writes full-time and lives in Arlington, Texas. She sings in a community chorus and loves to travel.

**PUBLISHER'S NOTE:** The following story has been thoroughly researched, and to the best of our knowledge represents a true story. While every possible effort has been made to ensure accuracy, the publisher will not assume liability for damages caused by inaccuracies in the data and makes no warranty on the accuracy of the information contained herein. This story has not been authorized or endorsed by Pitbull.

Blue Banner Biography

When Pitbull performs, he is confident and energetic. Here, he gets the crowd excited at the Major League Baseball All-Star Home Run Derby.

# Mr. 305

"*I* know you guys might be thinking, 'What is Pitbull doing here today?'" Pitbull said as he addressed the audience. "I'm thinking the same thing."

Armando Christian Pérez, or Pitbull as his fans know him, is famous for his rap and club music and high energy shows. But on this day in 2013, he is the opening speaker at the National Charter Schools Conference.

When Pitbull performs, his energy fills the room. He runs, jumps, and moves his body to the beat. He flashes a grin, winks his striking blue eyes, and laughs. But in front of the gathered charter school leaders and teachers, he is nervous. His passion for charter schools has pushed him outside of his comfort zone.

Some might say that because Pitbull's music is not written for kids or is not even good for them to listen to, he is not a good role model for charter school students. But others point to his life story as one that can inspire kids, especially at-risk kids.

Armando grew up in different parts of Miami, including an area called Little Havana. His family, like most in this neighborhood, came from Cuba. When Armando was in school, living with his mother, he thought selling drugs was an easy way to make money to get what they needed. But instead of continuing on this road, Armando found that he was good at rapping. He built a life for himself away from the dangers of drugs.

Even though he's recognized worldwide, he loves his hometown, Miami. He is even known as "Mr. 305" (305 is a Miami area code). He gives to charities and is involved in his community. For all his efforts, he was awarded the key to the city of Miami—one of his proudest moments.

> For Pitbull to discuss his personal life speaks to his commitment to charter schools. He rarely talks about his relationships.

"Pitbull not only lives in Miami but he's been traveling the country and the world sharing a positive message of Miami," Thomas Regalado, Miami commissioner, said at the ceremony. Pitbull summed it up by simply saying, "I'm very passionate about Miami."

The connection to Miami's charter schools is more personal. He reveals that three of his six children go to charter schools. "I'm not just a charter school advocate," he said in his speech at the National Charter Schools Conference. "First and foremost, I am a charter school parent. . . . Every day I see firsthand how my children are becoming highly motivated lifelong learners thanks to educators in the charter schools they attend."

For Pitbull to discuss his personal life speaks to his commitment to charter schools. He rarely talks about his relationships. "The only real thing in my life is real people in my life, so I'm very protective of them," he revealed to Ryan Seacrest.

Pitbull looks forward to the success of a new charter school that he helped launch called SLAM, Sports Leadership and Management, built in Little Havana. The curriculum prepares students for careers in sports (like medicine, business, or broadcasting), but also "entertains and engages" students in order to keep them interested in all subjects. Showing Neely Tucker of *The Washington Post* through the new school, Pitbull looked out the window of a SLAM classroom and pointed to downtown Miami.

"This isn't a trick—it's obtainable," he explained to Tucker. "I didn't grow up here seeing things that were so motivating or inspiring. Down there," he pointed at the street below, "you don't see the ways out."

*Pitbull performs one of his high-energy numbers at the iHeart Radio Ultimate Pool Party in Miami.*

Both of Pitbull's parents came to Miami from Cuba as young children. He's proud of his Cuban heritage and his Miami home. In 2009, he performed at the annual Calle Ocho festival in Miami wearing a shirt printed with the Cuban flag.

# Fight to the Death

Armando was born on January 15, 1981, in Miami. Both of his parents were from Cuba, where many freedoms disappeared after Fidel Castro took over. Armando's parents had been sent to the United States by their own parents.

His mother, Alysha Acosta, and his father, Armando Pérez Torres, were two of fourteen thousand children who were sent to the United States without their parents in the early 1960s in a program called Operation Pedro Pan. Because of Castro's strict rules, parents worried that the government would take their children away from them. They hoped their children would have a better life in America. Some had relatives in the United States, but other children had to go into foster homes. Alysha did not see her own mother for seven or eight years, Pitbull told David Letterman.

In 1980, Armando Sr. went back to Cuba to rescue other refugees during an event called the Mariel Boatlift. The economy had gotten so bad under Castro's rule that people were starving and desperate to leave. For a short time,

Castro allowed people to go. Boats were packed with Cubans crossing the Straits of Florida. In all, 125,000 refugees came to the United States. Shortly after Armando Sr. helped hundreds of these people escape Cuba, Alysha gave birth to Armando Jr.

> *Even though Armando was too young to understand what the poems were about, he learned that words could be powerful.*

When Armando Jr. was born, he already had five half-brothers and half-sisters. His father still loved Cuba and missed his country even though he knew living there was dangerous. "My father was very proud to be Cuban, so what he would do in order to instill those roots, is make me recite poems from José Martí," Pitbull recalled in an interview with VH1's *Behind the Music*.

José Martí was a Cuban poet who lived in the 1800s. He wrote about freedom and justice and his love for his homeland. Even though Armando was too young to understand what the poems were about, he learned that words could be powerful.

Life in Miami was hard, especially after Armando Sr. started selling drugs and drinking. He spent all the money he earned on drugs and alcohol. "It was . . . torture to see the man you love turn into—nothing," Alysha told *Behind the Music*. Alysha and Armando Sr. divorced when Armando Jr. was four. After that, he hardly ever saw his father. "We didn't have that [father figure in our lives]," Pitbull revealed to VH1. "That's where the hurt comes from, because you can't have a sense of attachment."

Alysha now worked two or three jobs at a time. "I struggled a lot to keep my family going," she confessed to VH1. "I would have done anything." But there was always the need for money. "She's the one that taught me how to look for that solution no matter what," Pitbull told *Behind the Music*.

In the 1980s, Miami formed its own style of hip-hop called Miami bass. Miami's music was faster and featured a heavy, syncopated bass. Technology made it possible for audiences to feel the bass vibrating in their bodies. By the late 1980s and early 1990s, songs like "Get It Girl" by 2 Live Crew, "Whoomp! There It Is" by Tag Team, and "Shake It" by MC Shy D were popular not just in Miami, but all around the United States.

Just as Miami's music influenced other artists outside of Miami, Armando was influenced by hip-hop music from

*Pitbull's early music was influenced by the music of Miami and the hip-hop from the rest of the country. His Cuban roots led to a combination of English and Spanish lyrics in his songs.*

around the country. He loved to beatbox. At an early age, he could produce beats and rhythms on the spot, using only his mouth and voice. When his sixth-grade music teacher gave out an assignment that required him to create his own music, he put his beatboxing talent to use. He impressed his teacher so much that he earned a "double A" on the project. In an interview with *Behind the Music*, Pitbull smiled as he recalled thinking, "Maybe we're on to something." He started freestyling, telling stories with his rhymes.

*He liked the challenge of the hustle and being able to handle anything that happened on the streets.*

Armando used street life as inspiration for his raps. Then he began to sell drugs himself because it was quick, easy money. "I'm watching all this go down but to me it's normal. To me, I'm thinking its how every kid grows up," Pitbull told VH1. He liked the challenge of the hustle and being able to handle anything that happened on the streets.

When his mother found out he was selling drugs, she was furious and kicked him out of the house. "I was not going to have a drug dealer for a son," she insisted to VH1. Pitbull told *Behind the Music*, "My mother always knew that in my blood I had a lot of my father. I was a go-getter, mover, shaker, loved the streets."

Deep down, Pitbull was angry at his father. He channeled all that anger into his music and became a relentless battle rapper—fighting other rappers with his rhymes. Armando was so good at battling that a friend began to call him "pit bull."

*Pitbull drew inspiration for his songs from the Miami neighborhoods that he grew up in.*

"When you talk about a pit bull, it has a very fierce reputation," Pitbull explained to *Behind the Music*. "But if you know about a pit bull, it's a very, very loving and loyal dog. Just like everything it depends on how it's raised. . . . it doesn't understand the word 'lose,' doesn't understand 'give up,' doesn't understand 'quit,' so when it fights, it fights to the death. But it feels like it's fighting for something. And what is it fighting for? Its owner. Well, my owner is life, and that's what I fight for."

He would need every bit of that determination to get off the streets and into music.

Pitbull earned his name and his reputation for his freestyles and
battle raps.

# Battle Rapper

*P*itbull's sister Perla Garcia told VH1, "[Armando] told me, 'A pit bull, when he bites down, he locks his jaw and he has it on lockdown.' And that's how he was going to have Miami one day."

Pitbull was still attending Miami Coral Park Senior High School during the day and dealing drugs on the streets at night. He would freestyle between classes and always drew a crowd. One day, Hope Martinez, the drama teacher, pushed through a crowd of students thinking she had to break up a fight. Instead she heard Pitbull rapping.

"He was amazing," Hope told *Behind the Music*. "To think that one can come up with the lyrics like that, on the spot, blew my mind."

She told Pitbull about a casting call for teenagers to appear as extras in a music video for rapper DMX. At the video shoot, Pitbull met DMX and other rappers from the Ruff Ryders crew. One of them, Drag-On, wanted to battle. Never one to back down, Pitbull went round-for-round with Drag-On and eventually won.

Irv Gotti, a record producer, approached Pitbull and asked him if he wrote music. When Pitbull said he only did freestyle, Irv pointed out that freestyle was okay, but songs made money.

"I started writing since that day forward," Pitbull explained to *Behind the Music*. "That's basically when it all started developing."

He began writing lyrics down and trying to shape them into songs. When he was satisfied, he got some money together and made a demo. His musical style contained elements of Miami bass and the southern crunk music that was beginning to gain popularity at the time. He also switched back and forth between English and Spanish. It was a unique sound in the rap world.

Luther Campbell heard Pitbull's demo and met him in person. He liked the drive he saw in the young man. Luther had been a member of the Miami bass rap group 2 Live Crew and now owned Luke Records. He signed Pitbull to a one-year contract, then arranged for him to go on a tour of the South. They would go to the local radio stations and lay down a challenge to rappers in the audience.

"I would take him in the hardest of the hardest 'hoods," Luther told VH1. "He's a white-looking Cuban guy and he's gonna battle whoever . . . bring your best."

Pitbull learned about the business, but he didn't earn much money. He sent most of what he did make home to his mother. Even though he was going to sleep hungry, he just couldn't give up.

Alysha told *Behind the Music* that she encouraged her son in those dark days. "You're going to be a star," she said to him. "Do it for mom." That always inspired him. "I was her last hope," he admitted to VH1. Pitbull was ready to work even harder.

But then Luther let Pitbull go. The clubs and radio stations weren't playing his songs. No one showed any

*Luther Campbell (left) signed Pitbull to a one-year contract, and worked to promote his music. Even though their partnership didn't work out, Pitbull and Campbell remained friends. They performed together with Trick Daddy (center) at the 2010 VH1 Hip Hop Honors.*

interest in his music. He ended up back home with little to show for all his effort.

Always looking for a way to pay the bills, he was tempted to go back to dealing drugs. "I've seen it destroy families, mine one of them," Pitbull told VH1. "But I looked at it where, as long as I'm disciplined, it will allow me to live."

Then, one night during a drug deal, his father saw what he was doing. Pitbull told *Behind the Music* that his father was concerned for him. "That right there — what I see you doing," he told Pitbull, "it's only going to take you two places: dead or in jail."

Even though he had talent, Pitbull struggled to find success in the music industry early on.

# From Negative to Positive

Armando Sr. gave Pitbull the guidance that he had been missing for so many years. Pitbull told VH1 that his father opened up to him. "I'm not going to talk to you like your father. I haven't been here like your father. I'm going to talk to you like a friend. And more than a friend, I'm going to talk to you like someone who knows exactly what you're doing and how you're doing it, and where it's going to go."

Not only did Armando Sr. give Pitbull advice, but he also wanted to have a place in his son's life again. Pitbull left the drug business for good and worked even harder at his music. He took inspiration from Jermaine Dupri's hit "Welcome to Atlanta," and turned it into "Welcome to Miami."

DJ Laz played "Welcome to Miami" on Miami's Power 96 radio station, and it became an instant hit. Pitbull began meeting people who could help him develop his music. After Lil Jon heard Pitbull's song "Oye" on the radio, he invited him to his studio to record. One of the short tracks that Pitbull recorded ended up on Lil Jon's album *Kings of Crunk*. Thanks to Lil Jon's encouragement, Pitbull began to use more Spanish in his songs. And his success began to attract interest from music labels.

He signed with TVT Records and in 2004, his debut album was released, called *M.I.A.M.I.: Money Is A Major Issue*. In 2005 he partnered with P. Diddy (Sean Combs) and Emilio Estefan to form the Bad Boy Latino record label. His connections were reaching farther in the music world.

As Pitbull developed his own style, he traded in his baggy clothes for tailored suits. His mother advised him not to look like "new money." Instead of wearing lots of shiny, expensive jewelry, Pitbull often chose just a classic watch or a pair of sunglasses to complete his look. He shaved off the hair that he had once worn in cornrows. He looked like the successful businessman that he was becoming.

Pitbull was happy that he had a relationship with his dad. "Getting to know my father filled a real big void inside

*As Pitbull worked harder, he began forming connections with music industry leaders. In 2005, he launched Bad Boy Latino with P. Diddy (right) and Emilio Estefan (center).*

of me," he shared with *Behind the Music*. "I was very strong, always a fighter, but very hurt inside. I was so caught up in disliking him that I really didn't give him a chance."

When his father found out he had liver disease and wouldn't live much longer, their relationship grew much closer. "I went from the kid needing love and affection from the father, to the father needing love and affection from the kid," Pitbull told VH1. He spent as much time with his dad as possible, taking him out to ride around the streets and beaches they loved so much. Pitbull wanted to make his father as happy as he could.

*Pitbull was happy that he had a relationship with his dad. "Getting to know my father filled a real big void inside of me," he shared with Behind the Music.*

Pitbull was on tour when he got the call that his father was dying. By the time he got home, Armando Sr. had already passed away. The next album Pitbull made was called *El Mariel*, named for the boatlift that his father had been involved in. He dedicated the album to his father.

Pitbull was more determined than ever. "I saw the look in his face that 'now I'm really going to take this thing to the next level, and I'm going to do it for my dad,'" DJ Laz told VH1.

Still Pitbull never forgot his roots. He honored his mother in the song "Castle Made of Sand" on his album *Planet Pit*. He acknowledges how hard life was for her. "I think that she feels I'm one of her only wins," he told *Behind the Music*, "but she's the reason I am who I am."

Pitbull reaches out to his hometown in many ways. Here he visits a patient at Miami Children's Hospital after performing for the hospital's patients as part of the Get Well Soon Tour.

# Mr. Worldwide

When Pitbull was a hungry, young artist, he was willing to do anything anyone said to find success. As time went on, though, he wanted more and more to take control of his own career. Like José Martí, the poet he recited when he was three, Pitbull wanted freedom to pursue his vision his way.

He had to go to court to get out of his contract with TVT. One of the biggest disagreements that Pitbull had with company executives was about working with other artists. He wanted the freedom to record and perform with anyone.

Once he was out of his contract with TVT, he began his own record label called Mr. 305 Inc. This change gave him the freedom to reinvent his music and his image, moving away from the hip-hop genre and into the world of pop, club, and party music. He also negotiated deals to endorse products and companies such as Dr Pepper and Kodak.

His new style reached a wider range of audiences, and he soon took on the title of "Mr. Worldwide." His tours are now global and so is his business. He works with musicians

*Pitbull likes to work with many different types of artists. Here, he performs the official 2014 FIFA World Cup song, "We Are One (Ole Ola)," with Jennifer Lopez (left) and Claudia Leitte (right).*

*Fans in Odemira, Portugal, cheer for Pitbull during his international tour.*

from all over the world who inspire him to take his music in new directions.

"Growing up around so many different people [in Miami] allowed me to think out of the box when it came to music," Pitbull explained to Lee Hawkins of WSJ.com. "And from a marketing standpoint, I mean, what better than to be able to be that bridge, that ambassador . . . to really show, literally, how powerful music is."

True to what he calls "the melting pot" of Miami, Pitbull's music keeps evolving thanks to the fact that he is open to music in all forms and from all artists. In 2014, he worked with Jennifer Lopez and Brazilian singer Claudia Leitte to record the official World Cup song "We Are One

(Ole Ola)." This performance will no doubt be followed by many more international projects. Pitbull's willingness to take his inspiration from anywhere helps him to maintain a rich environment for his creativity.

And there is always Miami, the city he loves. He finances social programs there and he is especially proud of the work he does with kids. "To me, the final chapter is to be able to give the youth that motivation, to inspire them. To me that's the revolution," Pitbull revealed to *Behind the Music*. "As much as it motivates them, it motivates me. Because I feel like I'm looking at myself in a lot of these kids."

Pitbull continues to reach out to the world, but he is grateful to those who supported him along the way. "I'm just blessed to be here. I celebrate every day. I'm a happy person. I'm not in the business of moving backwards, I'm in the business of moving forward," he told VH1.

> True to what he calls "the melting pot" of Miami, Pitbull's music keeps evolving thanks to the fact that he is open to music in all forms and from all artists.

Pitbull ends his concerts by saying, "*Dale!*" pronounced "DAH-ley." In Spanish it means something similar to "let's go," or "do it!" With that one word, he always seems to say, "if I can do it, you can do it." Dale!

**1981** Armando Christian Pérez Jr. (Pitbull) is born on January 15.

**1985** Parents Alysha and Armando Sr. divorce.

**1986** Miami bass group 2 Live Crew releases its first album.

**1997** Alysha throws Armando Jr. out of the house for selling drugs.

**2001** Luther Campbell signs Pitbull to a one-year contract.

**2002** Lil Jon includes "Pitbull's Cuban Rideout" on his album *Kings of Crunk*.

**2004** Releases first album *M.I.A.M.I.: Money is a Major Issue* with TVT Records.

**2006** Father Armando Sr. dies in May; releases *El Mariel*.

**2009** Gets out of his contract with TVT after a court battle; develops Mr. 305 Inc. under Sony Music.

**2010** Releases the all-Spanish album *Armando*.

**2011** Begins his first world tour, the Rebelution Tour, in Chile.

**2013** Becomes an official sponsor of SLAM, a charter school in Miami.

**2014** Pitbull, Jennifer Lopez, and Claudia Leitte release "We Are One (Ole Ola)," the official 2014 FIFA World Cup song.

2004    *M.I.A.M.I.: Money Is a Major Issue*
2005    *Money Is Still a Major Issue*
2006    *El Mariel*
2007    *The Boatlift*
2009    *Rebelution*
2010    *Armando*
2011    *Planet Pit*
2012    *Global Warming*
2013    *Meltdown*

## FURTHER READING

### Books

Cotts, Nat. *Pitbull*. Broomall, PA: Mason Crest, 2008.

Martí, José, and Esther Allen, trans. *Selected Writings*. New York: Penguin Books, 2002.

*Pitbull*. Costa Mesa, CA: Saddleback Educational Publishing, 2013.

### On the Internet

Billboard: "Pitbull"
http://www.billboard.com/artist/1490081/pitbull

Today: "Pitbull Gives a Tour of His Hometown"
http://www.today.com/video/today/50906938%20-%20
50906938#50906938

VH1: Behind the Music
http://www.vh1.com/shows/behind_the_music/series.jhtml

### Works Consulted

Associated Press. "Rapper Pitbull Gets Key to Miami." CBSNews, August 19, 2009. http://www.cbsnews.com/news/rapper-pitbull-gets-key-to-miami/

Cobo, Leila. "Bad Boy Latino Launches." *Billboard*, August 25, 2005. http://www.billboard.com/biz/articles/news/1407365/bad-boy-latino-launches

Cohen, Melanie. "Pitbull Released from TVT's Cage." *Wall Street Journal*, September 28, 2009. http://blogs.wsj.com/bankruptcy/2009/09/28/pitbull-released-from-tvt%E2%80%99s-cage/

Hawkins, Lee. "Pitbull the Mogul." WSJ.com, July 14, 2011. http://live.wsj.com/video/pitbull-the-mogul/328C0B26-334D-4525-9F5F-6958ABFE8DB9.html#!328C0B26-334D-4525-9F5F-6958ABFE8DB9

History. "Apr 20, 1980: Castro Announces Mariel Boatlift." *This Day in History*. http://www.history.com/this-day-in-history/castro-announces-mariel-boatlift

Jeffries, David. "Pitbull: Artist Biography." AllMusic. http://www.allmusic.com/artist/pitbull-mn0000350685/biography

Letterman, David. "Pitbull on David Letterman 26 November, 2013." YouTube video, 5:18, posted by "Tv Shows," November 26, 2013. http://www.youtube.com/watch?v=-nVd-X2kjrU

Marquina, Sierra. "Pitbull Dishes on Jennifer Lopez, Playing a Frog in 'Epic' . . . and Marriage." *On Air with Ryan Seacrest.* RyanSeacrest.com, May 21, 2013. http://www.ryanseacrest.com/2013/05/21/pitbull-divulges-everything-from-his-success-to-not-believing-in-marriage/

Operation Pedro Pan Group, Inc. "History." http://www.pedropan.org/category/history

Pitbull. "Pitbull Opens National Charter School Conference." YouTube video, 14:33, posted by "publiccharters," July 1, 2013. http://www.youtube.com/watch?v=b4vQ_9DwJCs

Sanchez, Claudio. "Is Pitbull 'Mr. Education'? Rapper Opens Charter School in Miami." *Code Switch*, NPR, October 15, 2013. http://www.npr.org/blogs/codeswitch/2013/10/15/234683081/is-pitbull-mr-education-rapper-opens-charter-school-in-miami

Sarig, Roni. *Third Coast.* Cambridge, MA: Da Capo Press, 2007.

Tarradell, Mario. "Pitbull: A Look at a Bling-less Rapper that Heeded Mama's Words and Forged an 'Old Money' Image." *Dallas Morning News*, June 17, 2013. http://popcultureblog.dallasnews.com/2013/06/pitbull-a-look-at-a-bling-less-rapper-that-heeded-mamas-words-and-forged-an-old-money-image.html/?nclick_check=1

Tucker, Neely. "Pitbull's School: Star Promotes a Radical Idea for At-Risk Kids." *Washington Post*, February 21, 2014. http://www.washingtonpost.com/lifestyle/magazine/pitbulls-school-star-promotes-a-radical-idea-for-at-risk-kids/2014/02/20/499db59c-854d-11e3-bbe5-6a2a3141e3a9_story.html

VH1. "Pitbull." *Behind the Music,* Episode 25, March 16, 2012. http://www.vh1.com/video/behind-the-music/full-episodes/behind-the-music-pitbull/1680810/playlist.jhtml

Vozick-Levinson, Simon. "Pitbull's Global Hustle Can't Be Stopped." *Rolling Stone*, November 22, 2012. http://www.rollingstone.com/music/news/pitbulls-global-hustle-cant-be-stopped-20121114

# INDEX